KNIGHTS

by Racquel Foran

Content Consultant
Andrew Holt
Associate Professor of History
Florida State College at Jacksonville

CORE
LIBRARY

Published by ABDO Publishing Company, PO Box 398166, Minneapolis, MN 55439. Copyright © 2013 by Abdo Consulting Group, Inc. International copyrights reserved in all countries. No part of this book may be reproduced in any form without written permission from the publisher. The Core Library™ is a trademark and logo of ABDO Publishing Company.

Printed in the United States of America,
North Mankato, Minnesota
112012
012013
♻ THIS BOOK CONTAINS AT LEAST 10% RECYCLED MATERIALS.

Editor: Lauren Coss
Series Designer: Becky Daum

Cataloging-in-Publication Data
Foran, Racquel.
 Knights / Racquel Foran.
  p. cm. -- (Great warriors)
Includes bibliographical references and index.
ISBN 978-1-61783-774-6
1. Knights and knighthood--Juvenile literature. 2. Civilization, Medieval--Juvenile literature. I. Title.
940.1--dc22
                                        2012946375

Photo Credits: Angus McBride/Private Collection/© Look and Learn/The Bridgeman Art Library, cover, 1; North Wind/North Wind Picture Archives, 4, 7, 8, 11, 16, 19, 21, 32, 36, 39; Dorling Kindersley RF/Thinkstock, 14; Photos.com/Thinkstock, 24, 27, 35, 45; Shutterstock Images, 28; iStockphoto/Thinkstock, 29, 40

CONTENTS

A CALL TO ARMS

In 1095 knights across Europe received a call to arms they felt they had to answer. These knights had thousands of men supporting them. The knights' blades were sharpened. Their armor was fitted and polished. They had stockpiled food. They had made their travel arrangements. They were ready for battle. They were ready for the Crusades.

The Crusades were a violent time in Europe. Many knights led armies south to take back formerly Christian lands.

On November 27, 1095, Pope Urban II urged European Christians to take back Jerusalem and other parts of the Holy Land. These lands had been Christian in ancient times. But people practicing Islam had taken over the lands. When the pope addressed the people, the knights answered his call.

Crusaders would be in the Holy Land for the next 200 years. They captured Jerusalem for a short time in 1099. But the Muslims who had previously controlled the city were angry that their land had been taken. In 1187 they recaptured Jerusalem. After years of violence and bloodshed, the formerly Christian territory remained mostly Islamic.

Religion in the Middle Ages

The Middle Ages in Europe lasted from about 500 to 1500. Many Europeans during the Middle Ages were Christians. In the late 1000s, Islam was expanding. Some European Christians were afraid Islam would spread into their territory.

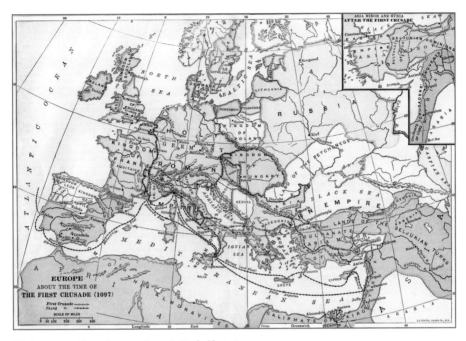

Europe During the Middle Ages

The crusading knights and their armies traveled thousands of miles to get to the Holy Land. This map shows some of the routes they took. What do you think the best land and sea routes would have been to travel? Looking at the map, what obstacles do you think the Crusaders encountered?

The church realized the knights could be used for religious purposes. But not all knights were religious like the knights who fought in the Crusades. Still, by the 1200s, religious and nonreligious knights began to play important roles in European society, politics, and warfare. The glory age of knights had begun.

THE HISTORY OF KNIGHTS

Knights were some of the best warriors of their time. Their primary job was to serve the upper class, usually a lord. They protected their lord's castle and carried out missions for him. In the early Middle Ages, men did not go through any formal training or ceremony to become knights. As late as the 1000s, knights did not come from the class they served. It took a few hundred years for knights'

Knights rode into battle on strong horses. They carried the best weapons and wore the best armor.

status in society to change. Eventually they went from regular soldiers to the noble heroes most people think of when they think of knights today.

Life in the Middle Ages

During the Middle Ages, Europe was covered with many different kingdoms, dukedoms, and principalities. The kings, dukes, and princes of these lands were constantly battling with one another. They wanted to gain more land and more power.

Chivalry

The Middle Ages are sometimes called the age of chivalry. The word *chivalry* was originally used to define mounted, fully armed cavalry. Over time the meaning of the word changed to refer to the code of conduct for all knights. This code included honor, loyalty, and courtesy.

These rulers gave land and privileges to local lords. A lord swore loyalty to his ruler in exchange for the land. He promised to go to war to protect his ruler's land when asked.

The peasants living on a fief farmed the land for the knight. A knight had legal rights over peasants on his fief.

From the 1100s on, lords relied on knights to protect their lands and castles. A knight would be given his own piece of land, called a fief. This made the knight a vassal, someone who is allowed to use a

Marrying Up

To get more wealth, knights often married the daughters of wealthy lords. A knight might even get his own fief through a smart marriage. William Marshal became a knight at the age of 21. He went to war a short time later. He fought well. But Marshal was still very poor. In 1189 Marshal married Isabel de Clare. She was the daughter of the Earl of Pembroke. After Clare's father died, Marshal became the Earl of Pembroke. He now controlled large amounts of land in Ireland and Wales.

piece of land in exchange for military service. Soon many knights became wealthy and powerful.

Knights Get More Power

Having land was important because it gave knights more authority. Owning land helped a knight make connections with noble families. It also gave a knight a source of income. Becoming a knight was very expensive. A knight had to pay for his weapons, armor, and horses. He also had to pay for the soldiers who fought for him, called retainers.

Knights who owned land became noblemen. Knights were fully a part of the ruling class. A boy could become a knight because his father had been one. A formal training process was established to train the sons of noble knights. By 1200 the noble warrior was common across Europe.

EXPLORE ONLINE

Chapter Two discusses the meaning of *chivalry*. Visit the Web site below to learn more about the idea of chivalry. Compare what you learn about chivalry on the Web site with what you have read about knights in this book. Do you think the knights' actions always lived up to the idea of chivalry? How did the meaning of chivalry change over time?

Chivalry
www.britannica.com/EBchecked/topic/11340 9/chivalry

CHAPTER THREE

BECOMING A KNIGHT

By the late 1100s, most knights had noble parents. And by this time, becoming a knight required a lot of hard work and training. For most knights, this training began at a very young age. They began training as young as age six.

A knight's training usually took about 14 years. A young knight spent his first seven years as a page. A page often served a knight. The page did simple

Becoming a knight meant many years of training.

A young knight-in-training began as a page, *right*, before becoming a squire, *left*, and finally a full knight, *center*.

tasks such as grooming the knight's horses or cleaning animal cages. Eventually the young page also began learning the skills he would need as a knight.

Life as a Page

A knight was a nobleman as well as a warrior. He needed to be able to manage his land. He was expected to have good manners. He also had to know about political issues. A page's education was well-rounded. Pages learned to read and write in their own language. They also learned Latin, the language of the Catholic Church. They learned about the Christian religion. They learned about personal hygiene and grooming. Knights were expected to be entertaining. Pages learned to play instruments or write poems.

A young knight had to learn how to ride on horseback. Pages rode ponies. They played games that acted out battles. Their weapons and shields were made of wood. These games prepared them for the next stage of their training.

Knightly Fashion

Knights were expected to know the latest fashions and dress accordingly. Pages learned about the current fashions during their training. Fancy clothes showed high social standing. Knights displayed their wealth with extra-puffy sleeves, large feathered hats, and big fur-trimmed cloaks. Clothes were also designed to show off a young man's muscular legs and broad shoulders.

Knights needed to be able to control a horse while charging at an enemy with a lance and a shield. Pages practiced riding their ponies while holding a wooden lance. A page practiced aiming his lance using a ring hanging from a tree. The page would ride toward the ring and drive his lance through it. Jousting was another important skill for an adult knight. To practice jousting, pages charged toward a scarecrow-like figure. This prepared them to ride against another knight later on.

Pages also spent long hours mastering their sword skills. They practiced sword fighting against wooden stakes. By the time a boy had moved from

One of a squire's many duties was to help dress the knight he served.

being a page to a squire, he was well on his way to becoming a knight.

Life as a Squire

After seven years as a page, a young knight became a squire. A squire served a knight. The squire lived in his knight's castle. He shared the knight's responsibility of serving a lord and other knights.

Squires were responsible for serving food and wine at banquets. They also made the knight's bed and helped him dress. Squires traveled to tournaments with their knights. During tournaments knights faced off against each other for a prize. A squire cared for his knight's horse. He made sure the knight always had the equipment he needed. If the knight went into battle, two squires fought beside him. They made sure the knight always had fresh horses and weapons.

Squires were skilled warriors by the end of their training. But not all squires became knights. A knight's equipment and armor was very expensive. Paying for the knighting ceremony was also very expensive. Many squires and their families could not afford it. Some squires stayed a squire for life.

The knighting ceremony was complicated and expensive.
Some squires never became knights because they could
not afford to be knighted.

Dubbings

Squires often had to pay for their own dubbing. Dubbings could be very complicated and expensive events. Squires prayed the night before their dubbing. The next morning, they took a bath before dressing in full armor. Then they received their sword and spurs. Most paintings and drawings of knightly dubbings show the knight being tapped on the shoulder with a sword. But a slap to the cheek was also common. Knighting ceremonies often included large celebrations with feasting and tournaments.

Knighthood

At the end of a squire's training period, he was ready to be knighted. In early times, this was nothing more than acknowledging that the boy had completed his education. Then he was given a sword and spurs and sent on his way. By the 1100s, knighting had evolved into a ceremony known as a dubbing. A formal gesture completed the ceremony. After 14 years of training, the squire was now a knight.

Geoffroi de Charny was a French knight who lived in the 1300s. He wrote several documents about being a knight. In the following passage, he discusses a knight's life:

> In this profession one has to endure heat, hunger and hard work, to sleep little and often to keep watch. And to be exhausted and to sleep uncomfortably on the ground only to be abruptly awakened. And you will be powerless to change the situation. You will often be afraid when you see your enemies coming towards you with lowered lances to run you through and with drawn swords to cut you down. Bolts and arrows come at you and you do not know how best to protect yourself. You see people killing each other, fleeing, dying and being taken prisoner and you see the bodies of your dead friends lying before you. But your horse is not dead, and by its vigorous speed you can escape in dishonour. But if you stay, you will win eternal honour. Is he not a great martyr, who puts himself to such work?

Source: Emily Sohn. "Medieval Knights May Have Had PTSD." Discovery News. Discovery Communications, December 20, 2011. Web. Accessed September 5, 2012.

Back It Up

Read the passage carefully. What main point is Charny trying to make? Write a paragraph describing Charny's main idea. Then write down two or three pieces of evidence that he uses to make the point.

CHAPTER FOUR

WEAPONS AND ARMOR

A knight had many weapons to choose from in battle. He needed to know how to use and defend against clubs, daggers, axes, spears, crossbows, lances, and swords. Each weapon had its own purpose. Losing a weapon during a fight was common. Knights always had multiple weapons to choose from during battle.

A knight needed to be skilled in fighting with each of the many weapons he might use in battle.

Tournaments

Tournaments were fake battles where a knight could show off his skills. The purpose was to disarm and capture an opponent, not to kill him. Tournaments helped keep a knight in fighting form. When tournaments were first held around 1100, the knight who fought the best would win a prize. A knight who won a tournament could also take his opponent's horses, armor, and weapons. The winner could force the loser to pay him for their return. By 1200 tournaments became events where a knight could gain wealth, respect, and fame. Only members of the nobility were able to compete.

Lances

A lance was one of a knight's most common weapons. Lances were wooden poles about 10 feet (3 m) long. One end of the pole had a metal tip. A knight tucked the lance firmly under his arm. Then, while riding his horse, he drove the lance at his enemy. The length of the lance kept a distance between the knight and his enemy.

Swords

Swords were another of knights' favorite weapons. Swords were very difficult to make

At tournaments, two knights charged at each other with their lances. The goal was to knock the other knight off his horse.

and very expensive to buy in the Middle Ages. They were often handed down from father to son for many generations. A sword was a knight's most treasured weapon. He almost always kept it by his side. Many knights used arming swords, which were carried with shields.

As sword-making technology improved, craftsmen were able to make longer swords. The long sword could be held with two hands. But it was light enough to hold with just one. It also had a sharp tip. A knight could thrust a long sword through armor.

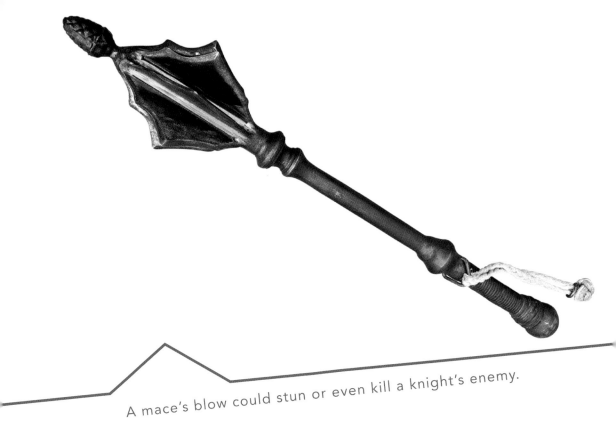

A mace's blow could stun or even kill a knight's enemy.

Other Weapons

The Middle Ages was a time of brutal warfare. Many knights fought with axes and daggers as well as swords and lances. Some knights used simple blunt weapons such as the club and the mace. A club could be made out of almost anything. But wood was most common. A mace was a far more lethal version of a club. Maces featured a heavy, spiked iron head attached to a wooden handle. A knight could swing the iron head to cut through armor.

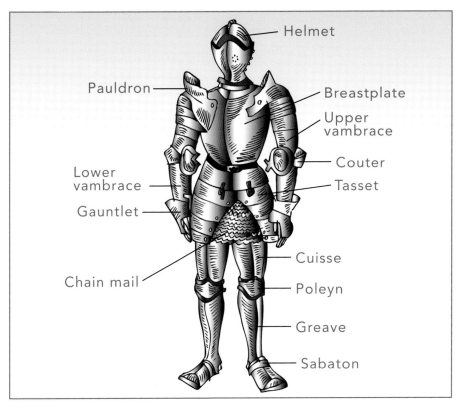

A Knight's Armor

Many pieces were involved in making a complete suit of armor. Some knights strapped on up to 20 pieces of steel plate. They could do this in as little as 15 minutes. Take a look at the armor above. Does it look light? Would it be easy to move around in? Do you see places it would be easy to slip in a weapon to wound the knight?

Armor

A knight needed to have good armor to survive the brutality of battle. But knights weren't always covered from head to toe in the plate armor people think of today. In the early Middle Ages, most knights wore chain mail. Chain mail was a well-fitted shirt with a hood. It was made of small metal rings.

Chain mail covered most of a knight's body, but it did not completely protect him. An arrow could pierce through the spaces between the rings. Mail also left a knight's legs exposed. Early knights wore helmets that were cone-shaped. A metal bar over the nose was the only face protection.

Armor began improving in the later Middle Ages. Knights began wearing helmets that hid their faces in the 1100s. By the late 1200s, knights were wearing steel knee plates. Over the next century, even more plating was added to a knight's armor. Soon knights were wearing visored helmets. This style of helmet completely covered a knight's head and face. The visor could be raised or lowered as needed. By the 1500s, knights were wearing full body armor.

A shield was another important part of a knight's armor. It protected him from flying arrows and swinging swords. It could also work as a weapon, delivering a heavy blow to an enemy. Shields were usually made of wood covered in leather. They varied in shapes and sizes.

FURTHER EVIDENCE

Chapter Four had a lot of information about knights, their weapons, and their armor. What was the main point of the chapter? What evidence supported the main point? Visit the Web site below to learn about new research on knights' armor. What new information can you learn from the Web site? Does the information you found support the evidence presented in the chapter? Or does it introduce new evidence?

History in the Headlines

www.history.com/news/in-shining-armor-medieval-knights-may-not-have-shone

CHAPTER FIVE

KNIGHT LIFE

A knight's duty was to protect what his lord had ordered him to protect. Knights defended towns, churches, and lords and their castles. However, some knights didn't serve a lord at all. Some knights served a group of knights.

Many knights were devoted Christians. Some of these religious knights began forming special groups called orders. These orders were modeled

A knight could serve more than one lord over his lifetime. But he usually served only one lord at a time.

Joan of Arc

In general women were not allowed to become knights. But one woman wore knights' armor and led an army. At the age of 13, Joan of Arc began to hear voices from saints. The voices told Joan that she must help Charles VII claim the French throne by defeating the English. Joan was just 17 years old when she led a small army of men into Orléans, France, in April 1429. Joan and her army captured the city. It was Charles's first victory. Charles was crowned king in July 1429. Joan was captured and handed over to the English less than a year later. She was burned at the stake on May 30, 1431.

after orders of monks. All members had been trained to be knights. To join an order, a knight took vows of poverty, purity, and obedience. He was expected to sacrifice his own needs to serve the order and the Catholic Church. Some of these orders engaged only in military activities. But most orders combined military activities with charity work.

Knights Templar

The first military order was the Poor Knights of Christ and of the Temple of Solomon, or

Although she was never knighted, Joan of Arc wore armor and fought with knights' weapons.

the Knights Templar. During the Middle Ages, it was common for people to go on a pilgrimage, or travel to the Holy Land. After capturing Jerusalem in 1099, some knights stayed there to protect holy landmarks and the pilgrims who also stayed.

The Knights Templar was one of the most well-known knightly orders.

A knight named Hugues de Payens led a group of knights who decided to live in Jerusalem. Payens's group became known as the Knights Templar. They lived in a strictly religious way. They were powerful fighters. But they were also committed to helping people. The church approved of the knights. In 1129 the church gave the knights official power to rule and keep order in Jerusalem. The church put the Knights Templar above laws. The knights answered only to the pope.

The new order soon became popular with other noble knights across the land. The Knights Templar were given gifts, privileges, and property in kingdoms across Europe. They soon became one of the wealthiest and most powerful orders of the time.

The Decline of Knights

By the 1300s, knightly orders had become very wealthy and powerful. Much of the ruling class was jealous of the knights' success. King Philip IV of France was particularly envious of the Knights

Knights of Legend

King Arthur and the Knights of the Round Table are some of the most well-known knights of history. Oral tales of Arthur first appeared as early as the 600s. These early tales evolved into popular French stories from the 1100s on. Arthur and his knights took part in great adventures. The tales of King Arthur and his knights were so popular that movies and books are still written about them today.

Templar. On October 13, 1307, King Philip had all Templars living in France rounded up and arrested. In 1312 Pope Clement V disbanded the Knights Templar. The Templar leaders who remained in France were killed.

New technology also added to the downfall of knights. By the 1300s, craftsmen in Europe were starting to create more modern weapons. Powerful new longbows were being used in combat for the first time. The first firearms appeared in the 1360s. Firearms were easy to use with little training. A knight's armor was no match for firearms. Military tactics changed. By the 1500s, knights were no longer

The stories of King Arthur and his Knights of the Round Table were some of the most popular legends of the Middle Ages.

very useful in battle. Knighthood became fully tied to social status rather than military abilities.

Knights Today

Knights haven't been used in battle for hundreds of years. But knights are remembered for their courtesy, bravery, and honor. People are still knighted today. But the title means something very different than it did during the Middle Ages.

The queen of England often knights people as recognition for performing a great deed or for charity

Some people show off their knightly skills at competitions and festivals, such as Renaissance fairs.

work. Modern knights don't need to have any military skills.

People still study the military skills knights used in the past. Special schools in North America and Europe teach jousting, sword skills, and other fighting techniques used by knights.

Knights still play an important role in popular culture as well. Many movies, books, and television shows feature knights. The last true warrior knight may have died hundreds of years ago. But the spirit of knights lives on in Western culture to this day.

STRAIGHT TO THE SOURCE

In 1130 Abbot Bernard of Clairvaux wrote a book on the Knights Templar called *In Praise of the New Knighthood*. In the passage below, he discusses the religious knights' ties to Christianity.

> *But the knights of Christ may safely do battle in the battles of their Lord, fearing neither the sin of smiting the enemy nor the danger of their own downfall, inasmuch as death for Christ, inflicted or endured, bears no taint of sin, but deserves abundant glory. In the first case one gains for Christ, and in the second one gains Christ himself. . . .*
>
> *The knight of Christ, I say, may strike with confidence and succumb more confidently. When he strikes, he does service to Christ, and to himself when he succumbs. Nor does he bear the sword in vain. He is God's minister in the punishment of evil doers and the praise of well doers. . . . Should he be killed himself, we know he has not perished, but has come safely home.*

Source: Bernard of Clairvaux, In Praise of the New Knighthood. *Trans. M. Conrad Greenia OCSO. Kalamazoo, MI: Cistercian Publications, 1977. Print. 39.*

Consider Your Audience

Read the passage above closely. How could you adapt Bernard's words for a modern audience, such as your friends or younger siblings? Write a blog post giving this same information to the new audience. How is the language you use for the new audience different from Bernard's original text? Why?

IMPORTANT DATES AND BATTLES

500s
The Middle Ages begin.

1095
On November 27, Pope Urban II calls on all Christian knights to fight to reclaim the Holy Land.

1099
The crusaders capture Jerusalem.

1200s
Noble knights become common across Europe.

1312
Pope Clement V breaks up the Knights Templar.

1360s
Firearms are first used in Europe.

1100s

Knights protect their lords' property. The knights are given fiefs in return.

1129

The Roman Catholic Church gives the Knights Templar power to rule and protect Jerusalem.

1130

Abbot Bernard of Clairvaux writes *In Praise of the New Knighthood.*

1429

In April, Joan of Arc leads a small army into Orléans, France. Joan and her army take the city in a major victory for Charles VII.

1430

Joan of Arc is captured and handed over to the English.

1500s

The Middle Ages end. The title of knight becomes tied to social status rather than military service.

STOP AND THINK

Say What?

Learning about knights can mean learning a lot of new vocabulary. Find five words in this book that you have never seen or heard before. Find out what the words mean and write the meaning in your own words. Then use the words in a new sentence.

Dig Deeper

What questions do you still have about knights? Do you want to learn more about their weapons? Or their training? Write down one or two questions that can guide you in doing research. With an adult's help, find a few reliable new sources about knights that can help answer your questions. Write a few sentences about how you did your research and what you learned from it.

Why Do I Care?

The Middle Ages may have been a long time ago. But your life may not be as different from a knight's as you think. Have you ever worked hard for a goal? Have you spent months or years training for a sport? What was it like? Write down two or three ways that this book relates to your life.

You Are There

Imagine that you are a page training to become a knight in the Middle Ages. Write 300 words describing your life. What is your day like? What is happening in your town? What is the best part of your life? What is your least favorite part of being a page?

GLOSSARY

abbot
the leader of a monastery

cavalry
horse-mounted soldiers

chivalry
courteous behavior
associated with the customs
of knighthood

dubbing
the ceremony of becoming a
knight

fief
a piece of land given to a
knight in return for service to
the lord of the land

page
a boy in his first stage of
training to become a knight

pilgrimage
a journey to the Holy Land as
an act of religious devotion

principality
a state with a prince as ruler

spurs
small devices that attach to
boots and can be used to
urge on a horse

squire
a teenage boy in the second
phase of his knightly training

vassal
a person granted use of land
in return for military service
to the landowner